What's a Synthesizer?

What's a Synthesizer?

By
Jon F.
Eiche

Simple answers to common questions
about the new musical technology.

HAL•LEONARD™
CORPORATION
7777 W. BLUEMOUND RD. P.O. BOX 13819 MILWAUKEE, WI 53213

ISBN 0-88188-671-8

Library of Congress Catalog Card No. 87-12149

First printing June, 1987

CONTENTS

Intro: *Do you need a Ph.D. in electrical engineering?*

UNLESS YOU'VE SPENT the last 20 years in a cave or on a desert island, you're aware that the march of technology has accelerated to a run. This has affected all areas of our lives, though perhaps none so strikingly as music. The new musical technology — **electronic** technology — amounts to nothing less than a revolution. Portable keyboards, for example, didn't even exist until the early 1980s. When they first came out, they were regarded as expensive toys. But by their sheer and unprecedented popularity, they have taken their place among "legitimate" musical instruments.

Even the tradition-bound world of Bach and Mozart has been affected. Interestingly, the electronic revolution transformed classical music even before pop music. The opening fanfares of this brave-new-world symphony were sounded in 1968, when Wendy Carlos' *Switched-On Bach* first appeared in the record bins. This one recording, realized entirely on a Moog synthesizer, and which sold more copies than any classical recording ever had before, proved to a disbelieving world that electronics could indeed produce **music,** and not just the "boops and bleeps" of popular fancy. Since then, use of electronic musical instruments by professional and amateur musicians alike has increased at an enormous rate.

Today synthesizers, portable keyboards, automatic drum machines, and more populate the world of electronic musical instruments. Even personal computers have gotten into the act. This fertile ground of new instruments and new ideas has stimulated crossbreeding between these species, with the result that the distinctions between them become fuzzier by the day. For example, portable keyboards, which initially borrowed heavily from electronic organs, have steadily taken on the characteristics of synthesizers.

Another by-product of the new musical technology is that equipment that does more than ever before now costs less than ever before. Professional-caliber instruments are within reach of the non-professional pocketbook. What's more, technology has elevated the mind and the ear to positions of greater importance than mere manual dexterity, opening the riches of music-making to those formerly denied access. This "democratization of music," as it has been called, is a dream come true for many would-be musicians. Perhaps you are one of them.

If there is a problem with any of this, it is the problem of ignorance and confusion: there seems to be so much to learn that it may overwhelm you. Never fear. You **can** learn enough to enjoy using this new musical technology, and you **don't** need a Ph.D. in electrical engineering to do so. This book will get you started.

Whether you are cautious and skeptical or curious and enthusiastic about the new musical technology, you'll find answers to your questions here. The pages that follow constitute a brief, understandable overview of the world of electronic sound. Things are kept simple enough so that you don't get lost, but you are told enough so that, should you wish to ask even more questions, you'll know how to ask them.

1: *What's a synthesizer?*

THE WORD "SYNTHESIZE" means "to put together." A synthesizer is a device that puts together the things that make up a sound. So in attempting to understand synthesizers, you must spend a little time getting to know what sound is about. Think about it for a moment: what is it that makes one sound different from another?

1. How can you tell the difference between a tuba note and a piccolo note?

2. What distinguishes a whisper from a yell?

3. Why does a saxophone sound different from a violin?

There are many subtle things that distinguish the sounds in the examples above; our ears can hear an astounding range of little differences, which is why it's possible to identify so many different sounds. But let's concentrate on the obvious for now:

1. A tuba note is **lower** than a piccolo note; this is a difference in **pitch.**

2. A whisper is **softer** than a yell; this is a difference in **volume.**

3. A saxophone sounds, well, **different** than a violin, even if they play the same pitches at the same volume. This is a difference in **timbre** (pronounced *"tam*-ber"), or tone color, and while it's a little harder to define, at least at first, than differences in volume or pitch, it's just as clear to our ears.

The three properties outlined in these three examples are the building blocks of all sound. These are the things that a synthesizer "puts together" in order to make different sounds. Now for a closer look.

SOUND WAVES

Have you ever stood next to a quiet pond and tossed a stone in, just to watch the smooth surface of the water break into a series of ripples? Sure you have. Think about exactly what happened: When the stone hit the pond, it upset more than just the water immediately around it, because *that* water in turn disturbed the water around *it*—and so on. The result was a series of ripples that spread out in ever-widening circles.

Sound is like that stone, and the air is like that pond. When something makes a sound, what it really does is vibrate, which you have felt if you have ever held your hand to your throat while speaking. That vibration causes a disturbance in the air, which spreads outward in ever-widening circles until it reaches your ear. Inside your ear, the disturbance in the air causes the eardrum to vibrate. That vibration is transmitted by an intricate array of connections to a set of nerve endings, which send a message to your brain that you interpret as "I hear something."

It's not a coincidence that we refer to "sound waves," a term that brings to mind a picture similar to the ripples in the pond. In a real sense, sound does consist of waves in the air — oscillations of higher and lower pressure. By connecting a microphone to a device called an **oscilloscope**, it is possible to see a picture of such sound waves.

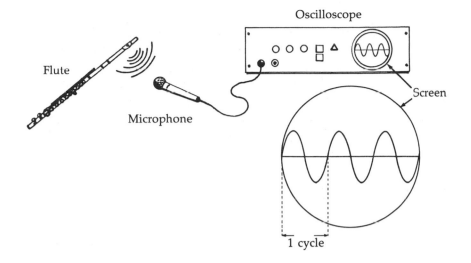

Looking at the picture on the oscilloscope screen, it is easy to grasp what happens in a sound wave: the air pressure alternately rises and falls repeatedly over time.

PITCH

Each repetition of a sound wave is called a **cycle.** The speed at which these cycles occur is called the **frequency** of the wave, and is measured, logically enough, in "cycles per second."

If you've ever driven a car, or a motorcycle, or ridden in a motorboat, or operated an electric mixer or blender in your kitchen, you have observed that the sound a motor produces changes depending on how fast it goes. Specifically, the faster a motor runs, the higher the pitch it produces. Motors, like sound waves, operate by making a series of repeated motions — cycles. A faster speed means more cycles per second. More cycles per second means a higher frequency. And, as your ears tell you when you step on the gas pedal in your car, a higher frequency means a higher pitch.

Low Frequency = Low Pitch

High Frequency = High Pitch

11

"Cycles per second," by the way, is often abbreviated "c.p.s." Another name for the same measurement is "Hertz," often abbreviated "Hz." It was coined in honor of Heinrich Hertz, a 19th-century German physicist who did pioneering work in the field of electromagnetic waves. One advantage of "Hertz" and "Hz" is that they lend themselves well to abbreviation; 1,000 Hertz, for example, can be written as 1 kiloHertz (1kHz), since "kilo-" is the standard scientific abbreviation for "thousand."

The human ear can hear frequencies between about 20 Hz (20 cycles per second) and 20 kHz (20,000 cycles per second). Below 20 Hz, the cycles are heard as separate events, and fail to "blur together" as a pitched sound. Above 20kHz, the waves simply move too fast for our ears to respond to. Dog whistles take advantage of a dog's ability to hear higher sounds than we can. The upper limit of human hearing tends to decline with age and with prolonged exposure to loud noise.

The following illustration shows the frequencies of some of the notes on a standard 88-key piano keyboard. Middle C is 261.6 Hz. The A above it, sometimes called "concert A" or "A-440," is 440 Hz. Every octave higher you go, you double the frequency (the A above A-440 has a frequency of 880 Hz); every octave down you go, you halve the frequency.

VOLUME

Now that you've mastered the horizontal dimension of the oscilloscope screen — frequency — you're ready to move on to the vertical dimension. The height of a wave, from top to bottom, is called "amplitude." It's related to the word "amplifier," and it pertains to **volume.**

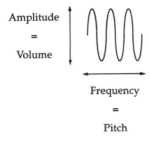

Amplitude = Volume

Frequency = Pitch

It's easy to understand why this is so: If something makes a small vibration, it creates only a small disturbance in the air. That small disturbance only vibrates our eardrums a little, and so we perceive it as a sound of low volume. But if something makes a big vibration, the disturbance of the air is large. It really rattles our eardrums, and the message to the brain is clear: "LOUD."

Low Amplitude = Soft

High Amplitude = Loud

Just as Hertz is the unit of measurement for frequency, so there is also a unit of measurement for volume: the decibel, abbreviated dB. Like Hertz, the decibel is named for a scientist: Alexander Graham Bell. Actually, the full unit of measurement is called a Bel; but since this unit was considered to large for the purposes of discussing the volumes of ordinary sounds, the decibel — a tenth of a Bel — was born.

It is worth noting a subtle distinction between Hertz and decibel: while Hertz is an objective measurement of an aspect of a wave (frequency), the decibel is a subjective measurement of the sound (loudness). Why is this so? Why not talk about measurements of amplitude, the actual height of a sound wave? Because it would be virtually meaningless.

Think about it: A jet plane produces quite "tall" sound waves. If you were standing on the runway next to a jet starting its engines, you would agree that it's loud. That's why the people who work around planes wear protection for their ears. But after the plane has taken off and is miles away in a matter of seconds, it's not so loud any more. Are the engines putting out smaller vibrations? No; they're just farther away. The moral of the story is, loudness is a relative matter.

Let's put loudness on a scale we can understand, as we did with frequency. 0 dB is called the "threshold of hearing"; it represents the softest sound you can hear. At the other end of the scale is the "threshold of pain" — sound so loud that it literally hurts — which is about 120 dB.

0 dB	Threshold of hearing; virtual silence
10 dB	Lightly rustling leaves
20 dB	Whispering
30 dB	Quiet traffic
40 dB	Full orchestra playing quietly
50 dB	Normal conversation
60 dB	Noisy office
70 dB	String orchestra playing loudly
80 dB	Full orchestra playing loudly
90 dB	Loud truck
100 dB	Heavy traffic
110 dB	Air hammer
120 dB	Threshold of pain; loud rock music

TIMBRE

So far we've dealt with two of the three properties of sound that were set forth at the beginning of this chapter: pitch and volume. And between them, they use up both dimensions of the oscilloscope screen: horizontal and vertical. Timbre is the aspect of sound that remains to be discussed, but it may not be clear where it fits into the picture. The answer lies in the **shape** of the wave — which is called, logically enough, the "waveshape," or "waveform."

The details of how different waveforms correspond to different timbres are beyond the scope of this book. For the purposes of this discussion it is enough to state a simple truth: a waveform with gentle curves will produce a sound with a somewhat dull, gentle timbre; a waveform with sharp corners will produce a sound with a bright, "sharp" timbre.

"Dull"   "Sharp"

Differences in timbre and waveform are the results of different **harmonics,** or **overtones,** in sounds. What are harmonics? Well, when you play a note on just about any musical instrument, what you hear is not actually a single tone, but a combination of different ones at different pitches and volumes. These are harmonics, and they are what enable you to tell a saxophone sound from a violin sound. Each musical instrument produces its own characteristic waveform (timbre), the result of a specific combination of harmonics — a "sonic fingerprint" that identifies it to the ear.

By the way, differences in timbre are also what enable us to understand human speech. This is what happens: The vocal cords produce a sound that is rich in harmonics. As the positions of our lips, tongue, and jaw change in forming syllables, they affect the relative volumes of those harmonics, strengthening some and weakening others. The results are audibly different vowel and consonant sounds.

15

2: *What is analog synthesis?*

THE BIRTH OF THE SYNTHESIZER came as musicians and electronics engineers pondered a practical way to create and control sounds — specifically, to control the three elements of pitch, volume, and timbre. What arose from these ponderings was a collection of related electronic devices, each of which performed a specific task. Originally, each of these devices was a separate module, so the synthesizers were called "modular." These modules were provided with some degree of control, and could be connected in various ways, giving them a certain amount of flexibility. (Connections between modules were made with "patch cords," and the results were called "patches" — terms borrowed form radio and telephone communications. The terminology has proven to be durable, for today, even though few synthesizers use patch cords any more, the control settings for a synthesizer sound are still called a "patch.") Since about 1970, more and more synthesizers have been manufactured as self-contained units rather than as collections of modules, trading flexibility for convenience. Nevertheless, the idea of separate, specialized functions remains.

PITCH

Since sound consists of waves, the basic component in the modular synthesizer is a wave-maker, called an **oscillator.** To further define its operation, it bears the full name **voltage-controlled oscillator,** or **VCO.** The abbreviation is just one of many spawned in the early years of synthesis; but the meaning is more important than the letters: Control of this module, and all others as well, is provided by changes of voltage — electricity. A simple yet versatile system. The waves that are produced by the oscillator are nothing more than variations in voltage. They are the electrical **analogs** — models, counterparts — of sound waves that travel through the air. Because the synthesizer produces and manipulates these electrical analogs directly, this kind of synthesis is called **analog synthesis.**

Some kind of controller, usually a keyboard, provides a control voltage to the oscillator, telling it what note to play. The earliest synthesizers could only play one note at a time; in the language of synthesis, they were **monophonic. Polyphonic** synthesizers — those capable of playing several notes at a time — were a later development. Most synthesizers now being made are polyphonic, though many have a monophonic mode, which is useful in certain circumstances.

MONOPHONIC   POLYPHONIC

17

VOLUME

With the means to produce electrical waves and control pitch, the next component to consider is the one that controls volume. This is the **voltage-controlled amplifier,** or **VCA.** The "voltage-controlled" part is as important here as in the voltage-controlled oscillator, for most musical sounds do not maintain a uniform volume for their entire length; rather, different sounds have different contours, or "envelopes." A few examples from the world of acoustical instruments will illustrate this:

- An accordion note begins slowly, because it takes time for the reeds to start vibrating. It builds to a certain level of volume, where it remains for as long as the key is held down and air is being squeezed through the bellows.

- A xylophone note starts quickly and fades away quickly.

- A piano note starts quickly and fades out gradually as long as the key is held down. When the key is released, the note ends quickly.

The synthesizer needs a means to produce different envelopes; the component that provides this means is the **envelope generator.** It allows the synthesizer player to establish the contour of the sound as a series of control voltages that regulate the voltage-controlled amplifier.

The most common envelope generator found in analog synthesizers divides the envelope into four different segments that can be controlled by the synthesist: Attack, Decay, Sustain, and Release. For this reason, this kind of envelope generator is usually called an ADSR.

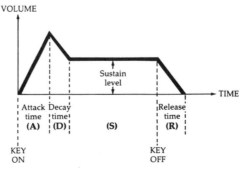

18

The attack segment governs the time it takes for the level to rise from 0 to an initial peak. Since many envelopes of acoustical sounds decay somewhat after the initial peak, the envelope generator includes a decay segment; as is the case with the attack segment, it controls a length of time. The decay segment ends at the sustain level, which is the level at which the sound remains for as long as the key is held down. After the key is released, the level returns to 0 at a rate determined by the release segment.

The keyboard sends a signal to the envelope generator to start the envelope; this signal, called a "trigger," is sent when a key is pressed. Another signal, called a "gate," tells the envelope generator to keep running until the key is released. The gate really **is** the electrical counterpart of a gate in a fence: it stays open (on) while the key is down. When the key is released, the gate closes, signaling the envelope generator to begin the release segment of the envelope.

Here's a diagram of the elements covered so far. As is the convention in block diagrams of synthesizers, arrows entering a block from below represent control voltages, and those entering from the left represent audio signals.

TIMBRE

A typical oscillator in an analog synthesizer offers a choice of several different waveforms for the production of different timbres. These waveforms are all simple shapes, and thus easy to produce as patterns of changing voltage, and yet they offer a broad variety of tone colors.

Further control over timbre is given by the **voltage-controlled filter,** or **VCF.** Like filters in the physical world, it screens out some elements while letting others pass. What it screens out are harmonics, which you may remember from Chapter 1. Because of the central role played by the filter in the removal of harmonics, analog synthesis is also know as **subtractive synthesis.**

The filter can be controlled by an envelope generator, just as the amplifier can. In this way, the timbre of a synthesized sound can change over time as the envelope generator changes the extent to which harmonics are filtered out. One example of this, so familiar that is has become a cliché, is the "wow" sound that is perhaps the sound most readily associated with the synthesizer.

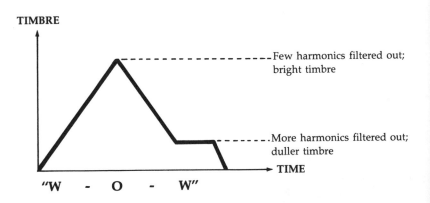

TIMBRE

Few harmonics filtered out; bright timbre

More harmonics filtered out; duller timbre

TIME

"W - O - W"

MODULATION

The typical synthesizer has other components designed to provide control over the sound. The most important of these is the **low-frequency oscillator,** or **LFO.** As its name implies, it produces waves at slow speeds (low frequencies) — usually below the audio range. It is used to change the output of the other components (oscillator, amplifier, filter); this kind of change is called **modulation.** When the low-frequency oscillator is used to control the main audio-frequency oscillator, it results in **vibrato,** or **frequency modulation,** which is a repeating variation in pitch. You've probably seen a violinist produce vibrato by moving his or her left hand back and forth on a string while playing.

When the low-frequency oscillator is used to control the amplifier, the result is **tremolo,** or **amplitude modulation.** This is a repeating variation in volume. The most familiar examples of tremolo are the rotating speakers used with electronic organs, and the motorized "fans" found on vibraphones.

The low-frequency oscillator can also be used to control the filter, which is called simply **filter modulation.** This is similar to a harmonica player wiggling his hand across the back of his instrument, creating an alternation between a muted and an unmuted sound.

The low-frequency oscillator has two basic controls: speed and depth. They correspond to the frequency and the amplitude of the low-frequency wave. Since the latter control is especially useful in performance in order to add and remove modulation, it has come to be included on many keyboard synthesizers as a small wheel, placed at the left end of the keyboard, that can be rotated by the thumb or fingers of the left hand while playing. It's usually called the **modulation wheel,** or **mod wheel.**

PUTTING IT ALL TOGETHER

Here is a block diagram of the main components of the analog synthesizer as it has been outlined on the previous pages. Be aware that this actually represents only the minimum standard components of a typical analog synthesizer. Many synthesizers, for example, have the capability of combining two or more audio-frequency oscillators to produce a sound. But what is covered here is enough to give you a solid fundamental understanding of how synthesizers work.

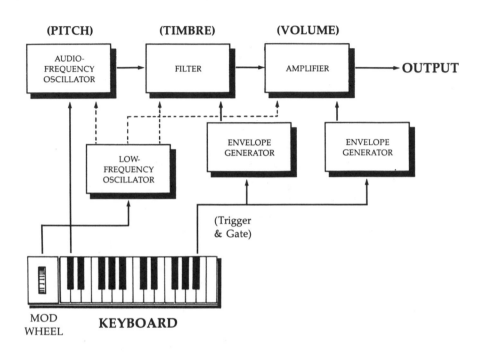

Although digital synthesizers (see Chapter 4) have claimed much of the popularity that once belonged to their analog cousins, analog synthesis remains the best place to begin learning about the use of electronics in music, for at least three reasons:

1. It is important historically as the starting point of the new musical technology.

2. It divides synthesis into logical areas that are directly related to the three components of sound (oscillator=pitch, filter= timbre, amplifier=volume).

3. Because of reasons 1 and 2 above, many digital synthesizers are patterned after the classic analog model. And analog synthesizers themselves have refused to die out completely.

3: *Does "a velocity-sensitive multitimbral keyboard with a programmable split point" really mean anything?*

BEFORE THE ADVENT of voltage-controlled synthesizers, an earlier generation of electric and electronic instruments had been developed, such as the Hammond organ and the Rhodes electric piano, with the intent of providing economical and, in some cases, portable alternatives to traditional instruments. The sounds of these instruments were approximations, at best, of their acoustical counterparts. In fact, their most prominent features were their idiosyncracies and shortcomings: a noticeable click at the beginning of each note in the case of the Hammond, and a thick, bell-like timbre in the case of the Rhodes.

Then something odd happened. Over the course of years of being played in concerts and on recordings, the "Hammond sound" and the "Rhodes sound" (to remain with these two examples) became desirable. When the Hammond Organ Company changed the technology in its instruments and did away with the previously unavoidable "key click," many performers were outraged. Public demand forced the company to find a way to "put the click back" into later instruments.

There is a parallel between these earlier instruments and the synthesizer. Although the designers of the modular synthesizers of the

1960s didn't conceive of them for the purpose of imitating acoustical instruments, performers soon began seeking ways to make the synthesizer an imitative instrument. The sounds they developed, though they were poor imitations, became trademarks, so to speak, of the "synthesizer sound." And when newer, digital synthesizers were developed (see Chapter 4), they were judged on their ability to reproduce sounds such as "analog strings" and "synth brass" — as well as, not surprisingly, the Hammond organ and the Rhodes electric piano.

CONTROLLERS

Whether synthesizer designers and players agreed on imitative synthesis or not, both groups saw the need to make synthesizers **expressive,** in order to make them truly **musical** instruments. This has already been seen in the discussion of envelope generators in Chapter 2. So the designers developed a number of different kinds of controllers to make this possible.

Since most synthesizers are played from a keyboard, it was natural that on many of them the keyboard was given a sensitivity to touch similar to that of the most familiar keyboard instrument: the piano. This kind of touch-sensitivity is called **velocity-sensitivity,** for changes in sound are a result of the **speed** with which the key is pressed.

Another kind of touch-sensitivity is **after-touch,** or **pressure,** sensitivity. This allows the player to control the sound after the key has been pressed, while it is being held down.

VELOCITY (SPEED)

PRESSURE (FORCE)

VELOCITY-SENSITIVE   PRESSURE-SENSITIVE

Complete control over pitch is essential to expressiveness on most acoustic instruments. A guitarist or a clarinetist shapes the pitch of a note every bit as carefully as he or she does the volume or the timbre. Consequently, nearly every keyboard synthesizer includes a controller to obtain pitches that the keyboard alone cannot. This is the **pitch-bend** control. It may take any of a number of physical forms, including a wheel (similar to the modulation wheel), a lever, a joystick, or a touch-sensitive ribbon. The pitch-bend control usually is placed with the modulation wheel at the left end of the keyboard; together, these two are often referred to as the **left-hand controllers.**

Pitch-Bend Wheel

Modulation Wheel

TYPICAL LEFT-HAND CONTROLLERS

Another means of controlling pitch is **portamento,** sometimes called **glide.** This is usually used in monophonic mode (when the synthesizer can only play one note at a time), and it works this way: When the player connects the notes — pressing each successive key down before releasing the previous one — the pitch slides from the former note to the latter one. But when he or she plays the notes separately, they sound separately, with no slide between them. A control governs the speed of the portamento.

Wind controllers are another class of control devices. The simplest of these are small mouthpieces that connect by wire to the synthesizer and respond to breath pressure. Both hands are left free to play the keyboard and operate other controllers. More elaborate wind controllers are not so much supplements to the keyboard as alternatives to it. The most famous of these is the Lyricon, which looks like and is played as a soprano saxophone. There are also trumpetlike wind controllers. In all these cases, the synthesizer itself is separate from the controller.

The idea of separating the control of the synthesizer from the electronics is one that exerted a strong appeal to keyboard players in rock bands during the 1970s. Hidden behind increasingly large stacks of instruments, they envied the freedom of the guitarists to move about the stage and capture the attention of the audience. Consequently, a few adventuresome players began using portable "strap-on" keyboard controllers. And it should come as a little surprise that some of these players, such as Jan Hammer, became known for a style of playing that imitated the guitar, especially in its use of the pitch-bend control. (This serves to make an important point about imitative synthesis: Convincing imitation depends as much on duplicating the playing style of an instrument as it does on reproducing its timbre.)

STRAP-ON
KEYBOARD
CONTROLLER

Once synthesists began pretending they were guitarists, it wasn't long before guitarists wanted to be synthesists. Guitar controllers existed during the 1970s, but it wasn't until MIDI arrived in the 1980s (see Chapter 7) that they began to become widely accepted. Then the same technology that allowed guitarists to control synthesizers also allowed all other instrumentalists, and even vocalists, to do the same.

It seems that some players want to take advantage of every available part of the body in controlling the synthesizer. So foot controllers are also made, and they range from simple on-off pedals similar to the sustain pedal on a piano to full control panels for the feet — often used by guitar synthesists. There are also pedal keyboard controllers, similar to the bass pedals on organs.

BASS-PEDAL
CONTROLLER   ELECTRONIC DRUMS

Electronic drums compose another class of synthesizer controllers. Although the drum pads were initially connected to a special synthesizer that produced only percussion sounds, new technology and new players have begun to blur the distinctions between keyboards and drums.

OTHER ELEMENTS

In addition to the voltage-controlled oscillator, which produces simple waveforms, most analog synthesizers include a **noise generator,** which produces sound without any specific frequency, or, more precisely, sound in which all frequencies are present in equal amounts. It is useful in creating many special effects that would otherwise be impossible to produce. This noise, which sounds something like radio static, is also called "white noise." When it is filtered to emphasize or eliminate certain frequencies, the result is "colored noise." It is not unusual for synthesists to speak of "pink" or "blue" noise!

Some synthesizers use technology to help play themselves. One component used for this purpose is the **arpeggiator,** which, when more than one note is being played at one time, causes the notes to sound one after the other (an arpeggio) rather than simultaneously. A related device, the sequencer, is discussed in Chapter 6.

There sometimes is confusion about the word "voice" as it is applied to synthesizers. Synthesizer designers prefer to use the word to describe the "polyphony" of an instrument: a 16-voice instrument is one that can play 16 notes at one time, for example. On the other hand, players often use it as a synonym for "patch" — a specific sound. To avoid confusion, it might be best to use "patch," or its equivalents, "preset" and "program," when talking about sounds.

Some synthesizers are able to play more than one patch at a time. These instruments are known as **polytimbral,** or **mutlitimbral.** The simplest of these play one patch in one part of the keyboard and another in the other part. These are known as **split** keyboards. On some, the player can determine where one patch stops and another starts; these instruments are said to have a **programmable split point.** Some keyboards can be split into more than two parts. More sophisticated keyboards can assign a different patch to each voice (that is, each note played); on such a synthesizer, playing four notes at a time can result in each sounding in a different timbre.

Just as a **split** keyboard plays different patches on different keys, a **layered** keyboard plays different patches on the same keys, at the same time. This allows the synthesist to play more than one "instrument" at the same time. Often, two versions of a single patch are layered, with one of them **detuned** — tuned slightly higher or lower than normal; the result is a fuller sound.

SPLIT KEYBOARD

LAYERED KEYBOARD

MICROPROCESSOR CONTROL

As mentioned before, the earliest analog synthesizers were modular, and produced different sounds by means of patch cords and the setting of numerous switches and dials. Such instruments are still being made and used, but in increasingly smaller numbers. The primary drawbacks to them are that it takes time to change from one sound to another, and it is not always possible to produce the same sound twice in a row, since analog controls incorporate a degree of uncertainty.

29

These drawbacks were overcome for the first time in the late 1970s, when **microprocessors** were introduced to the synthesizer world. A microprocessor is essentially a tiny calculating machine (smaller than the nail on your little finger), capable of performing rapid numeric operations, such as adding, subtracting, and comparing numbers. Microprocessors made synthesizers **programmable** — capable of making changes to patch settings easily, then storing those settings so that the entire patch could be recalled at the touch of a button. On such a synthesizer, when the synthesist makes a change to a patch, he or she is said to be **editing** it, or **programming** the synthesizer.

Some people refer to the microprocessor as the "CPU" ("Central Processing Unit"); others call it a "computer brain." But the microprocessor by itself is not quite a complete computer. A **program,** which is simply a set of instructions, is necessary to tell the microprocessor what operations to perform. This program is stored in memory — usually a kind of memory that can't be changed, so the program can't accidentally be erased. This kind of memory is known as **ROM.** That acronym stands for "Read-Only Memory," meaning the microprocessor can only "read" instructions from it; it can't "write" any instructions into it.

Patches in a programmable synthesizer are stored in a kind of memory that **can** be changed. This kind of memory is properly called "read-write memory," because the microprocessor can both "read" from it and "write" into it; but it is more popularly known as **RAM** ("Random-Access Memory"), because RAM and ROM sound good together. RAM requires electrical power to retain what is stored in it, so programmable synthesizers are equipped with a battery that serves as a backup power supply when the synthesizer itself is turned off.

Many synthesizers have some sort of **interface** — a technical word for "connection" — that allows patches to be stored outside the instrument. This storage allows the player to assemble a "library" of sounds, more than could possibly fit in his instrument at one time. Depending on the instrument, storage may be on cassette tape, floppy disk (similar to magnetic tape, but in the shape of a disk; storage and retrieval are faster than with tape), or a RAM cartridge that can be plugged into the instrument. Instruments that use RAM cartridges usually also have ROM cartridges available, containing patches that have been developed for commercial sale.

STORAGE MEDIA (L-R): Cassette Tape, Floppy Disks, RAM Cartridge

Because microprocessors deal with numbers, the adjective **"digital"** is frequently used when speaking of the things they do. The digital world — the world inside the computer — is a world of discrete divisions and separate steps. A digital clock, which contains a simple microprocessor, displays the time as definite numbers. In contrast, the analog world — the world around us — is a world of continuous change. An analog clock — the familiar one with the circular face and the sweeping second hand — shows not only the hours, minutes, and seconds, but all of the infinite times in between them. An analog synthesizer typically uses continuous controls (called "potentiometers," or "pots") to provide settings for the oscillators, filter, and so on; when programmability (microprocessor control) is added to such an instrument, the settings must be converted into numbers for storage in RAM. The result is a loss of the subtlety of continuous control, but a gain in preciseness and the ability to reproduce a patch exactly.

An analog synthesizer controlled by a microprocessor is known as an **analog/digital hybrid.** In addition to programmability, the microprocessor can perform other functions, including keeping oscillators in tune and "scanning" the keyboard to determine when keys are pressed or released. The logical step beyond the analog/digital hybrid is the completely digital synthesizer, in which even the generation and manipulation of the sound are accomplished digitally. This is discussed in the next chapter.

4: *How does digital synthesis work?*

A PURELY DIGITAL SYNTHESIZER puts the microprocessor in charge of virtually every aspect of control. The difference between this kind of instrument and an analog/digital hybrid is the way the sounds are generated. A digital synthesizer begins with a series of numbers, rather than an actual electrical wave. These numbers, which are stored in memory, **represent** a wave; each number represents the amplitude — the height — of the wave at a certain point in its cycle. The microprocessor is responsible for reading the numbers from memory, one by one, and then sending them out to be assembled into a wave. The speed at which the numbers are sent out determines the frequency of the wave. This is the digital counterpart to the voltage-controlled oscillator, and in fact some digital instruments use the label "DCO" ("Digitally Controlled Oscillator").

At some point, the numbers must be translated into voltages, for it is electrical current that runs a loudspeaker, allowing the synthesized sounds to be heard. This is accomplished by a **digital-to-analog converter,** or **DAC**.

Since the numbers that the digital synthesizer uses to represent a wave are separate, discrete steps, and since they are produced at separate, discrete intervals of time, the output of the digital-to-analog converter resembles a staircase, rather than the smooth, continuous motion of the analog synthesizer.

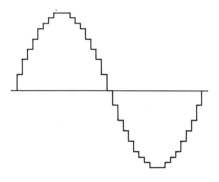

DIGITAL WAVEFORM

Just as a digital wave looks different than an analog wave, it also sounds different. The sharp corners of the "steps" result in additional high harmonics. The easiest way to remove those harmonics is with a filter. This "smooths out" the wave.

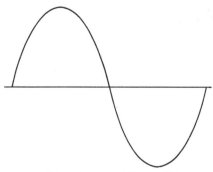

FILTERED DIGITAL WAVE

Digital synthesis is not limited to the simple waveforms of analog synthesis. Producing different waveforms is simply a matter of generating different combinations of numbers.

ALGORITHMS

There are many different methods of digital synthesis, and it seems that instruments employing "new and improved" methods appear every year. These different methods are sometimes called **algorithms,** a word that means roughly the same things as "procedures," or "recipes." What follows is a discussion of the most prominent of these.

Wave-table synthesis relies on lists, or **tables,** of numbers stored in memory. Each table contains the numeric representation of a different waveform. To generate a given waveform, the microprocessor sends out the numbers from the appropriate table. Some wave-table synthesizers seek to unite the advantages of digital and analog by combining complex digital waveforms and conventional analog filters.

Additive synthesis, also called **harmonic** synthesis, produces different timbres by combining (adding) waves at various pitches and volumes. Each of these waves represents a single harmonic.

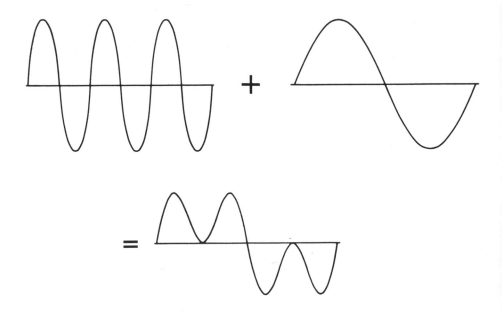

Additive synthesis is also known as "Fourier synthesis," after the 19th-century French physicist who first discovered that complex waves can be described as combinations of simple waves. Sophisticated applications of additive synthesis allow the simple waves to change independently over time — not only in volume, but in some cases in pitch as well, if desired. Such instruments place a high degree of expressive control at the synthesist's disposal, but require an equally high degree of skill to program, not to mention a great deal of time.

Another algorithm of digital synthesis, which may be called additive in a more general sense of the word, involves combining two or more **complex** waveforms. Changes in timbre result from changes in the relative volumes of the component waves.

FM (frequency modulation) synthesis is a widely used algorithm for digital synthesis. The idea of frequency modulation was introduced in Chapter 2, with the example of a low-frequency oscillator modulating an audio-frequency oscillator. When the frequency of the modulating wave (the low-frequency wave) is below the audible range of 20Hz, the result is vibrato — a wavering of pitch.

MODULATOR   CARRIER

RESULT

But when the frequency of the modulating wave is raised into the audible range, it affects the timbre (the waveform), rather than the pitch, of the wave being modulated. The standard term for the modulating wave in FM synthesis is "modulator"; the term for the wave being modulated is "carrier."

MODULATOR   CARRIER

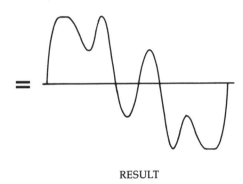

RESULT

Both additive synthesis and FM synthesis are possible on analog synthesizers, but benefit from the precise control available on digital instruments.

Waveshaping synthesis, also known as **nonlinear distortion** synthesis, is another useful digital algorithm. In this algorithm, a simple wave is "distorted," or "bent," into a different waveform.

It is worth noting that digital technology has not replaced the analog synthesizer — any more than one algorithm of digital synthesis can replace another. Different kinds of synthesizers are good for producing different kinds of sounds. Analog synthesizers are known for producing "warm, fat" sounds. Digital synthesizers excel in producing "clean, sharp" sounds. The kind of synthesizer you choose to play depends on the kind of sound you want. Many musicians choose to play several different kinds of synthesizers in order to have different kinds of sounds available to them.

5: *Why is digital sampling so popular?*

FOR MANY PEOPLE, the sounds of acoustic instruments are more satisfying than those of synthesizers. They are the sounds they grew up with, so they are more familiar. In addition, they are inherently more interesting than many electronic sounds because they are more complex and capable of greater variety.

On the other hand, electronic instruments offer several advantages, such as stability of tuning, portability, low price, and connection to sequence recorders for note-perfect performances (see Chapter 6).

Some new musical instruments seek to unite the benefits of acoustic sounds and electronic control. The primary means of doing so is **digital sampling,** often called merely "sampling."

Sampling can be understood as the digital recording of a sound. This is essentially the reverse of the production of a sound in a digital synthesizer:

The sound starts in the real world as a sound wave. It is converted to an electrical wave by a microphone. The amplitude (height) of this wave is measured at regular intervals of time. Each of these measurements is called a **sample** (although, by extension, the entire sampled sound is often referred to as a sample, too). These sampled electrical voltages are converted to numbers by an **analog-to-digital converter (ADC).** The numbers are stored in memory.

The numbers can be turned back into sound by exactly the same method that digital synthesizers use: a digital-to-analog converter changes the numbers to voltages, then a filter smooths the rough edges, and finally an amplifier and speaker system convert the electrical current into sound.

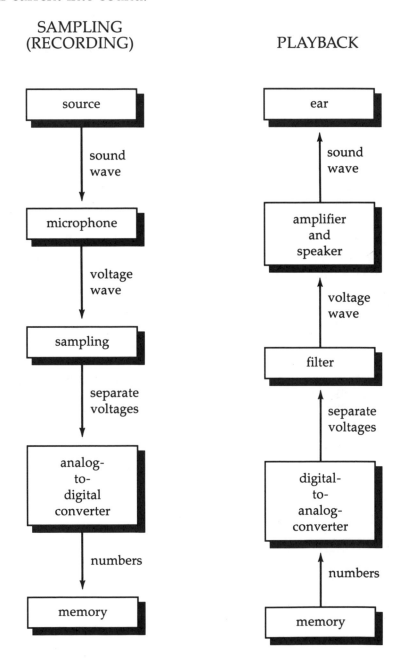

SAMPLING
(RECORDING)

PLAYBACK

MULTI-SAMPLING

It would seem that, as in digital synthesis, one sampled sound could be made to generate an entire musical scale merely by being played back from memory at different speeds. Played back slowly, it would produce a low pitch; played back quickly, it would produce a high pitch. And this is correct, as far as it goes. But for reproducing the sounds of acoustic instruments, it fails to take an important fact into consideration. High and low acoustic sounds are not merely fast and slow versions of the same waveform.

For example, if you take a recording of a man singing and play it back twice as fast, it doesn't sound like a man singing an octave higher; it sounds like a chipmunk! In fact, this is how the many "chipmunk" recordings of the 1950s and '60s were made. They used ordinary analog tape recorders, but the principle applies to digital sampling as well.

THE "CHIPMUNK EFFECT": One sample does *not* fit all.

The way to overcome the "chipmunk effect" is to use samples of different pitches, rather than a single sample at different speeds, to construct a musical scale. This is known as **multi-sampling.** (It usually is neither necessary nor practical to sample every pitch of the scale; to conserve memory, most multi-sampling instruments rely on a smaller number of samples, taken at different points in the scale, which are sped up and slowed down to produce the pitches in between.)

Another use of multi-sampling involves sounds of different dynamics. To use the familiar example of the piano, consider a single note being played twice — first softly, then loudly. The difference in sound is actually much more than just "soft" versus "loud." The softer tone is also more muted than the loud tone; stated another way, the loud tone is brighter, has more high harmonics. In order to reproduce this kind of variety, samples taken at different dynamic levels are necessary.

Multi-sampling also allows samples of different sounds to be assigned to different keys, or even to the same key. In this way, the sounds of flute, string orchestra, and guitar (for example) might be played from a single keyboard at one time.

An important technique for conserving memory, and hence cost, in a sampling instrument is **looping.** As the name suggests, this involves storing only a short segment of a sound, which is played over and over again when a long sound is called for, rather than recording the original sound in its entirety.

RESYNTHESIS

One of the shortcomings of sampling is that, unlike synthesis, the sound is fixed — it cannot be changed. This can be overcome, to some extent, by putting the sampled sound through filters, envelope generators, and such, but there are limits to what these add-ons can accomplish. "Wouldn't it be wonderful," you might say, "if I could start with the sounds of the real world, such as sampling provides, and then change anything about them, as I can with a synthesizer."

You have probably guessed by now that such a thing is not at all impossible. The solution lies in what is called **resynthesis.** What this means is that the sampled sound is analyzed by a computer and "translated"—resynthesized—into an algorithm of digital synthesis. Additive synthesis is the algorithm usually used. From this point, you can change any aspect of the sound, just as you can with any other sound constructed by additive synthesis. In a sense, resynthesis fulfills the promise made by sampling: the uniting of acoustic sounds and electronic control.

6: *What do all those other boxes do?*

SYNTHESIZERS AND SAMPLING INSTRUMENTS are only the beginning of the equipment that is related to making music with the help of electronics. You can bring many other devices into play. The most fundamental of these are amplifiers and speakers, since many synthesizers do not have them built in. And if you play more than one electronic instrument at a time using a single sound system, you also need a **mixer** to combine the sounds. Many times small mixers are built into multitrack cassette tape recorders, resulting in what amounts to a portable recording studio.

EFFECTS

On the subject of sound, there are many different **effects** devices, sometimes called **signal-processing** devices, available to enhance the sound of the music you produce. Many of these use digital technology to combine high performance, flexibility, and low cost. **Reverberation,** or "reverb," units add a feeling of resonance to the sound, such as is produced in a concert hall. **Digital delay lines** (DDL's) are used for a variety of effects, including chorus (the illusion of several instruments playing the same part) and echo (different from reverb in that it consists of discrete repetitions of the sound; reverb is less distinct, more of a "wash" of sound).

REVERBERATION   CHORUS   ECHO

Equalizers allow you to emphasize or de-emphasize certain ranges of frequencies; they're essentially refinements of the "Bass" and "Treble" tone controls found on many home stereos. **Noise gates** cut out any sound below a certain level of volume. These are often used when recording with microphones, to eliminate background noise, but have a special application in contemporary "techno-pop" music: When used in conjunction with reverb, they produce a sound that is both resonant and "dry," since, when the reverberation descends to a certain level, it cuts off abruptly rather than trailing off naturally. The classic example of this gated reverb, as it is called, is the sound of Phil Collins' snare drum.

GATED REVERB

A **limiter** does the opposite of a noise gate: it cuts out sounds **above** a specified level of volume. A related device is the **compressor,** which "evens out" the overall volume by increasing the volume of soft sounds and decreasing the volume of loud ones.

Panning devices are used to cause the sound to shift back and forth between the right and left stereo channels. **Pitch transposers,** also called **pitch shifters** and **harmonizers,** can change the pitch of a note. They have a number of uses. When the pitch shift is slight, the shifted note and the original note can be combined for a thick detuned effect. The shift can also be to another note entirely, so that the original and shifted notes together produce two-part harmony. Some harmonizers are capable of producing harmony in several parts at one time.

The **vocoder** can make a musical instrument such as a synthesizer "speak" or "sing." It does this by superimposing the timbre (the vowels and consonants) of a vocal sound onto the pitch or pitches of an instrumental sound.

INSTRUMENTS

The separation of synthesizer keyboards from their sound-producing hardware, mentioned in Chapter 3, led to the commercial production of **remote keyboard controllers,** which produce no sound of their own, but rather are used to play external synthesizers. Some of these controllers are portable "strap-on" models, while others are full-size keyboards.

The remote keyboard led naturally to a complementary device, the **expander module,** or **tone module,** which is an electronic musical instrument "in a box"—that is, without a keyboard of its own. Many of these modules are made to be mounted in a standard rack designed for audio components.

FACEPLATE OF A TYPICAL SINGLE-HEIGHT RACK-MOUNT MODULE
(Approximately 19" x 1¾")

Part of the attractiveness of using electronic technology to make music lies in the ability to play things you wouldn't otherwise be able to play. This is the function of the **sequence recorder,** or **sequencer,** which is perhaps the cornerstone of the "democratization of music" mentioned at the beginning of this book.

When analog synthesizers were in their prime, a sequencer consisted of a bank of adjustable controls that could produce a repeating "sequence" of notes. Each control specified the pitch of a single note, and so the number of notes in the sequence was limited by the expense and impracticality of a large number of controls. With the introduction of microprocessors, the number of notes that the sequencers could produce expanded greatly, since the information for playing each note could now be stored in memory, and no longer required a separate control for each note. Furthermore, these digital sequencers allow you to record directly from the synthesizer. Most offer a choice of recording in **step mode** (specifying each note individually) or in **real-time mode** (live).With a sequencer you can record slowly and play back at a faster speed without changing the pitch, because you are recording **musical information** (note on, note off, etc.) rather than actual sounds. You can change patches during playback, if you wish. And if your sense of rhythm is less than perfect, you can use **auto-correction,** sometimes called **quantization,** to line everything up with the beats. Some advanced sequencers even allow you to perform "microsurgery" on your music, lengthening a note here, changing a pitch there.

RECORDED SEQUENCE BEFORE QUANTIZATION

SAME SEQUENCE AFTER QUANTIZATION

Sequencers are available both as **hardware** (separate, stand-alone devices) and as **software** (programs that run on general-purpose computers).

Remote keyboards, expander modules, and sequencers have mush-roomed in popularity since the advent of MIDI (discussed in the next chapter), as have **drum machines.** A drum machine essentially combines a special sequencer and the electronics necessary to pro-duce percussion sounds. Increasingly, a kind of sampling known as **Pulse-Code Modulation (PCM)** is used to generate these sounds. The way drum machines work, percussion **patterns** of one or two measures' length are linked together into **songs.** There usually is a variety of patterns stored in ROM, and you can also program your own patterns, using either real-time mode or step mode, as with a sequencer.

7: *What is MIDI?*

IN 1981, DAVE SMITH, President of Sequential Circuits, delivered a proposal at the convention of the Audio Engineering Society for what he called the Universal Synthesizer Interface (USI). This proposal was based on discussion among several manufacturers of electronic musical instruments. Further discussion and modification of the proposal resulted in agreement in 1982 for what was now called **Musical Instrument Digital Interface,** or **MIDI.** The details were ironed out by 1983, when the "MIDI 1.0 Specification" was published. It was the birth of a new era in music, considered by many to be as important as the development of the analog synthesizer in the mid-1960s.

MIDI is the glue that holds modern musical electronics together. "Interface," as mentioned earlier, means "connection." It also means communication. What MIDI does is allow instruments made by different manufacturers to "talk" to one another. In fact, the original purpose of MIDI was simply to allow two synthesizers to be connected so that you could press a key on one and have both play. That it does, and much more, as you'll find out. But before discussing what MIDI does, let's take a look at what it is.

WHAT MIDI IS

On the surface, MIDI is easy to define: it consists of cables that plug into musical instruments and related equipment. The standard MIDI cable has a five-pin plug on each end:

These plugs fit into what are called MIDI **ports.** There are three different ports possible (though not all MIDI equipment has all three), labeled IN, OUT, and THRU:

IN receives MIDI information from other equipment.

OUT sends MIDI information to other equipment.

THRU provides a duplicate of the information received by IN, to be passed along to other equipment.

The "MIDI 1.0 Spec," as it's called, gives requirements for the electronics hardware necessary to make MIDI work as well as outlining the MIDI language. That language consists of numbers (remember: **digital** interface) that can be interpreted and acted upon by the microprocessors in electronic musical instruments.

WHAT MIDI DOES

The simplest use of MIDI is to control a synthesizer remotely. To do this, a MIDI cable is used to connect the OUT port of one synthesizer to the IN port of another. This is called a "master-slave" setup.

Playing the keyboard of the "master" will cause the "slave" to sound as well. It is important to reemphasize that what is sent over the MIDI cable is **information (data),** not sound. In fact, the usefulness of this kind of setup lies in having each instrument produce a different sound, resulting in a true instrumental ensemble.

A MIDI master-slave setup can also consist of a remote keyboard controller and an expander module, or a sequencer and a synthesizer or other MIDI-equipped instrument. For the purposes of both recording and playback with a sequencer, the IN and OUT ports of both units are used:

Using the THRU port of the slave allows more slaves to be added in series. This is known as **daisy-chaining:**

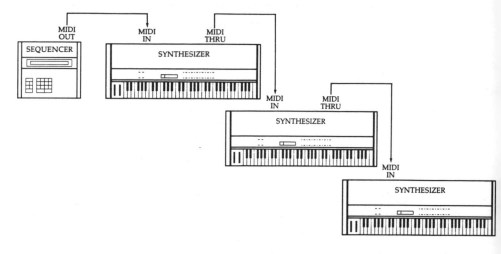

But daisy-chaining is not without problems; after two or three slaves, the MIDI information can undergo some distortion, with the result that further slaves in the chain may not play accurately. The solution to this lies in the use of a **MIDI THRU box,** which produces several parallel THRU signals from one IN:

MIDI CHANNELS

Picture this: You've recorded an entire symphony into a MIDI sequencer and have connected a dozen slaves to play the parts—synthesizers, sampling instruments, expander modules, electronic pianos, electronic organs, and portable keyboards. Everything's plugged in, turned on, and ready to run. In nervous anticipation, you press START on the sequencer, and all your instruments start to play. But wait! They're all playing the same part!

Clearly, MIDI sequencing would be severely limited if there weren't some way of directing different parts to different instruments. The authors of the specification foresaw this, and included such a means of separation: MIDI **channels.**

MIDI channels can be compared to TV channels: an instrument has to be "tuned" to the correct one or it won't receive what is being transmitted. There are 16 channels available, and each one can transmit any number of notes to any number of instruments. To return to our example of the symphony, you could record the flute part on channel 1, and set an appropriate sampling instrument to that channel for playback; if the string parts were on channel 2, you might set three different expander modules to that channel, detuning them slightly for a fuller sound and setting one to play an octave higher than the others; if the trombone part, using the pitch bend control for its many slides, were on channel 3, you could set a synthesizer to that channel with the appropriate patch; and so on. Any or all MIDI channels can be transmitted over a single MIDI cable.

As you can see, combining MIDI sequencers and instruments amounts to having a tapeless recording studio!

There is one more item to be added to the discussion of channels: a thing called **Omni** mode. Omni mode means that the instrument in question will receive on all MIDI channels at the same time. (Note that Omni mode involves receiving MIDI information; nothing **transmits** in Omni mode.) Some instruments cannot be set to Omni mode; others cannot be set to anything else.

MORE THAN NOTES

From what has been said about Omni mode you can see that, although MIDI is a standard, different instruments **implement** it to different degrees. How do you know what areas of the specification a MIDI-compatible piece of equipment does and doesn't implement? Read the **MIDI Implementation Chart** that comes with it. Every piece of MIDI equipment has one of these.

Manufacturer		Model	
		Version	Date

Function		Transmitted	Recognized	Remarks
BASIC CHANNEL	Default			
	Changed			
MODE	Default			
	Messages			
	Altered			
NOTE NUMBER	True Voice			
VELOCITY	Note On			
	Note Off			
TOUCH	Key's			
	Chan's			
PITCH BENDER				
CONTROL CHANGE				
PROGRAM CHANGE	True #			
SYSTEM EXCLUSIVE				
SYSTEM COMMON	Song Pos			
	Song Sel			
	Tune			
SYSTEM REAL TIME	Clock			
	Messages			
AUX	Local Control			
	All Notes Off			
	Active Sense			
	Reset			
NOTES:				

Mode 1: OMNI ON, POLY Mode 2: OMNI ON, MONO O: Yes
Mode 3: OMNI OFF, POLY Mode 4: OMNI OFF, MONO X: No

A BLANK MIDI IMPLEMENTATION CHART

MIDI information covers much more than just "note on, note off." Provisions have been made for velocity and aftertouch information, used by touch-sensitive keyboards. Most instruments include recognition of MIDI **program changes,** so that when you activate patch number 5 on the master, patch number 5 on the slave will also be activated. (Once again, it is not the **sound** that is transmitted; for example, on the master, number 5 might be a synthesized piano sound, while on the slave it might be a sample of a quacking duck.) Pitch bend is another area of the specification, as are controllers, such as sustain pedal and mod wheel.

IMPORTANT WARNING: Beginning users of the MIDI often don't realize that **MIDI can't make an instrument do something it wasn't designed to do.** For example, most electronic pianos don't implement pitch bend. So even if you slave such an instrument to a synthesizer and use pitch bend on the synthesizer, the electronic piano won't bend. Similarly, instruments that are not multitimbral won't magically be able to play several sounds at once merely because they're slaved to a multitimbral master, and so on.

MIDI sequencers and drum machines usually implement the MIDI **timing clock,** so that one such instrument in a setup can be designated the master and the other(s) the slave(s), synchronized to it.

Although most of this book has been devoted to synthesizers and sampling instruments, MIDI opens the marvels of technology to **all** musicians. Many electronic organs and portable keyboards are now equipped with MIDI. MIDI guitar controllers are marketed by several companies. There are MIDI modifications available for acoustic pianos. There are even pitch-to-MIDI converters, which allow singers and players of acoustic instruments to participate.

Much equipment other than musical instruments is also MIDI-compatible. Audio effects devices and mixers are one prominent category. There are also MIDI lighting controllers. There is a growing number of MIDI processing devices, such as programmable THRU boxes, data filters, and channel changers ("channelizers," they're called). And then there are computers; but more on these shortly.

SYSTEM EXCLUSIVE

There were precedents for MIDI in interfacing systems developed previously by several synthesizer manufacturers (in fact, modular synthesizers, by definition, required communication among several units), but these worked only with equipment of one given brand. As mentioned before, the idea behind MIDI is communication between instruments of any make. But the designers of the specification saw that it would also be useful for instruments of a given brand to be able to exchange information that pertained only to that brand or that model. They allowed for this in MIDI, by a capability called **system exclusive.**

System exclusive information is used mostly to transmit patch settings (or sampled waveforms) between instruments. It also is used to "dump" the memory contents of one sequencer (or drum machine) to another of the same kind. And it has applications in some computer programs designed to work with specific instruments.

THE COMPUTER CONNECTION

The digital messages of MIDI are made to order for personal computers, which contain microprocessors just as electronic musical instruments do. So it should come as no surprise that a great number of MIDI products have to do with computers.

THE COMPUTER
The ultimate MIDI device?

Two things are necessary in order for a computer to "speak MIDI." The first of these is the proper interface. Yes, you're right, MIDI **is** an interface, but since most computers don't have MIDI ports built in (a few do), they require some sort of adaptor (an interface, in other words) in order to connect to MIDI cables. The second thing necessary is the proper **software,** or **program.** The personal computer is a kind of a blank slate; it can't do anything at all until it is told what to do and how to do it. Software is what tells it. There are several kinds of MIDI software available for personal computers:

Patch librarians allow you to assemble a "library" of sounds for your synthesizer. The patches are transferred between synthesizer and computer using system exclusive information. Patches can be arranged and rearranged easily with the advantage of being able to see them listed on the computer screen. (The screen is one of the single most important assets of the personal computer, since it shows more information than the displays in most "dedicated" musical instruments can.) Libraries are stored on disk or cassette tape, depending on the computer.

Patch editors, or **voicing programs,** allow you to edit voices with the help of the computer. Again, system exclusive information makes it possible; and again, the screen makes the job easier than it would otherwise be. Some of these programs go so far as to "invent" new patches for you.

Waveform editors are the equivalent of patch editors for sampling instruments. Waveforms can be cut, spliced, looped, redrawn, and more.

Drum machine pattern editors allow you to compose and alter percussion patterns for drum machines with the help of the computer.

Sequencers offer capabilities comparable to dedicated hardware sequencers.

Song albums are arrangements of music, usually played in conjunction with a specific software sequencer. The advantage of these over conventional recordings is the same as that of other sequences: the ability you have to change anything about the performance (tempo, sounds, number of parts, etc.).

Music printing (scoring) programs give you "sheet music" from the computer printer. Often these, too, work with a software sequencer.

Telecommunications programs allow you to send and receive MIDI information over the phone. Patches, samples, sequences, and more can be exchanged this way.

Education. Many programs are available, covering all aspects of music, from "What is a treble clef?" to "Trumpet fingering."

Coda: *Where do we go from here?*

PREDICTIONS ARE ALWAYS DANGEROUS. No one knows for certain what technological marvels await the musician of the future. Ease of use and quality of sound probably will continue to increase, and price-to-performance ratios continue to become more attractive. But exactly what we can expect to see, no one really knows.

Despite all the change and uncertainty, one thing will remain constant: Music will always be a means for people to express themselves. For you, that may mean writing a computer program that composes music by itself; it may mean strumming a guitar and singing folk songs; it may mean MIDIing two portable keyboards together and playing Broadway show tunes.

It is **not** necessary to have the latest technology in order to make satisfying, expressive music; the piano is several hundred years old, and remains a superlative musical instrument. True, technology can help. If you play the guitar but dream of having an orchestra at your disposal, MIDI is for you. If you want to play music but you're all thumbs, sequencers are for you. If you'd like to practice the drums but don't want to disturb the neighbors, electronic drums are for you. Just remember: The pieces of equipment are only tools. What is most important is **you.** Make music! Express yourself! There is no substitute for that, and there never will be.

Index

guitar controller, 27, 53, 57
Hammer, Jan, 26
Hammond organ, 23-24
hardware, 46
harmonics, 15, 20, 33, 34
harmonizer. *See* pitch shifter
Hertz (Hz),12
Hertz, Heinrich, 12
implementation chart, 52
interface, 30, 47, 55
key click, 23
keyboard, 17, 19, 24, 44, 46, 49, 53
    strap-on, 26, 44
kilo-, kiloHertz (kHz), 12
layered, 28-29
left-hand controller, 25
librarian, 55
library, 30, 55
lighting controller, 53
limiter, 43
looping, 40, 55
loudspeaker. *See* speaker
master, 49, 53
memory, 32, 37, 38, 39-40, 54.
    See also RAM, ROM
microphone, 10-11, 37-38, 43
microprocessor, 29-31, 32, 45, 54
Middle C, 12
MIDI (Musical Instrument
    Digital Interface), 27, 46, 47-56, 57
mixer, 42, 53
modulation, 21, 35
    wheel, 21, 53
modulator, 35
monophonic, 17, 25
Moog synthesizer, 7
multi-sampling, 39-40
multitimbral, 28-29, 53
multitrack tape recorder, 42
music printing, 56
noise, noise generator, 28

noise gate, 43
Omni mode, 52
oscillator, 16, 19, 22
    audio-frequency, 22, 35
    digitally controlled (DCO), 32
    low-frequency (LFO), 21, 35
    voltage-controlled (VCO), 16, 32
oscilloscope, 10-11
overtones, 15
panning, 43
patch, 16, 28-29, 31, 51, 53, 54, 55, 56
patch cord, 16, 29
patch editor. *See* voicing
    program
patch librarian. *See* librarian
pattern (drum machine), 46, 55
piano, 57
pitch, 9, 11-12, 16-17, 22
pitch-bend, 25, 51, 53
pitch-shifter or transposer, 43-44
pitch-to-MIDI converter, 53
polyphonic, polyphony, 17, 28
polytimbral. *See* multitimbral
port, 48, 49, 55
portable keyboard, 7-8, 53, 57
portamento, 25
potentiometer ("pot"), 31
pressure-sensitivity, 24, 53
processing device, MIDI, 53
program, computer, 28, 30, 54-56, 57
programmability, 28, 30, 31, 34
pulse-code modulation (PCM), 46
quantization, 45
rack-mount, 44
RAM (Random-Access
    Memory), 30-31
real-time mode, 45, 46
remote keyboard controller. *See*
    keyboard
resynthesis, 40-41

ABOUT THE AUTHOR

Jon Eiche has served as a writer and editor for Hal Leonard Publishing since 1980. In this capacity, he has worked on owner's manuals and other books for Yamaha, Casio, Roland, Kurzweil, and numerous other manufacturers of electronic musical instruments. A self-confessed "keyboard klutz," he frequently applies his knowledge of musical technology in performance at local churches with his wife, a singer.

He also moonlights as a music critic for *The Milwaukee Sentinel,* and has assembled and edited *The Bach Chaconne for Solo Violin: A Collection of Views* for the American String Teachers Association.